The Good News about Heaven

*A Collection of Thoughts
from a Renowned Pastor*

· · · · · · · · · · · ·

Charles L. Allen

A Barbour Book

*Dedicated to the loved ones
of those who read this book.*

All Scripture is from the King James Version of the Bible.

Copyright © MCMXCV by Barbour and Company, Inc.

ISBN 1-55748-599-2

Published by   Barbour and Company, Inc.
              P.O. Box 719
              Uhrichsville, Ohio 44683

Printed in the U.S.A.

Contents

· · · · · · · · · · · ·

The Good News About Heaven
• • •

5
• • •

Introduction

· · · · · · · · · · · ·

Three Views of Heaven

Our first thoughts of heaven are of a place with gates of pearl, streets of gold, and angels singing. When we are young, we are inspired by the beauty of God's home. We can relate to the small girl who looked with wonder at the star-studded sky and exclaimed, "If the wrong side of heaven looks like this, what must the right side look like?"

As time goes by, we come to that moment when a loved one has died. Heaven takes on an entirely new meaning because that dear one is there. As years go by, we experience the death of other loved ones, such as a father or mother, brother, sister, child, spouse, and dear friends. Many people live to the time when more of their loved ones are in heaven than on earth. Heaven becomes the place where our loved ones are rather than the place with the pearly gates and golden streets. We understand Thomas Moore's words in "Come Ye Disconsolate": "Earth has no sorrows that heaven cannot heal."

As we grow older, we realize increasingly that our lives on this earth are not forever. We think more of our own eternal home. Many of us have seen demonstrated in the lives of others William Shakespeare's words, "The love of heaven makes one heavenly."

Gotthold Lessing once said, "A single grateful thought toward heaven is the most complete prayer." I hope this book will support and expand your thoughts of heaven.

To Mildred F. Parker, I express grateful appreciation for her help in editing this manuscript.

Charles L. Allen

1

· · · · · · · · · · · ·

We Live Not Twice,
but Three Times

The meaning of life, both physical and spiritual, is inextricably entwined around the fact of death. At death the soul, freed from the pains, weariness, ills, and limitations of the body, begins its highest life. Death is the beginning of the higher life.

Actually, we live three times: twice on this earth and once in the world to come. The first life on earth is before birth, and it prepares us for our second life. Our eyes and ears are formed so that after birth we can see and hear. The brain is formed to give us the ability to think and reason in the second life. Feet and legs develop so that after birth we can learn to walk. Through study of the first life, we can know much about what the second life will be like.

The second life, the one on this earth, likewise has its greater meaning in the next life, or the third life, the one after death. In the third life our

The Good News About Heaven
• • •

spiritual eyes are opened and our spiritual ears
are unstopped. The relation of the first to the second life is comparable to the relation of the second to the third life. Each prepares for the next;
each is the fulfillment of the one before.

Life in the womb would be incomprehensible
if there were no birth and life on earth. Likewise,
immortality gives us understanding of the unan-
swered questions from life on earth and makes
the earthly life comprehensible.

Birth and death are similar experiences: Both
involve passage from the known to the unknown—the sudden ending of the only life one
knows—and a drastic change in the atmosphere.

Suppose an unborn baby could be told of the
life it would live after birth. With an undevel-
oped mind and understanding, the fetus would
feel dread and fear. The prophet Isaiah realized
a similar experience occurs when we are born
into the next world. Paul later quotes Isaiah: "But
as it is written, Eye hath not seen, nor ear heard,
neither have entered into the heart of man, the

things which God hath prepared for them that love him" (1 Corinthians 2:9, Isaiah 64:4). Before birth and before death, the imagination is equally almost helpless.

However, the baby does not enter this world totally unprepared. Its arms and legs are made to move, its eyes to see, and its ears to hear. The body of the newborn baby is capable of growth and development by adjusting to its new environment. Likewise, our spiritual facilities will adjust to the third life and we will experience unending growth and development. Death is merely a physical occurrence.

The baby is expected before it is born and, in a nurturing environment, preparations are made. A crib and tiny clothes are purchased or received and, most importantly, loving, caring hearts are anticipating the baby's birth. Likewise, Jesus said, "I go to prepare a place for you" (John 14:2). We do not enter the next life as strangers. We are expected and prepared for. We are eagerly desired.

Just as birth is necessary to the second life, so death is necessary to the third. In this world the body is the house of the soul. By our bodies we are known and distinguished; indeed, no two people have identical fingerprints. Likewise, we shall be known as ourselves in the third life. "For now we see through a glass, darkly; but then face to face: now I know in part; but then shall I know even as also I am known" (1 Corinthians 13:12).

One of our difficulties is we look at the unborn child in retrospect and we look at the next life in the future. We can see backwards, but forward is not so clear. However, both birth and death are the continuance and fulfillment of life. Actually, they are both the same: death to the old world, birth to the new.

2

. . . .

All Christians Believe
in Immortality

You cannot be a Christian and not believe in immortality. When one believes in God, in Jesus Christ, in the Holy Spirit, and the communion of saints, belief in life everlasting logically follows. The Christian view of life is not a dead-end street.

Through the centuries people have asked the question of God that Job asked: "If a man die, shall he live again?" (Job 14:14). Some of us are content to get all we can out of this life and not think about eternity.

Others, on the other hand, have been so unhappy in this life they will be glad when it is over. The poet A. C. Swinburne composed these lines:*

> *From too much love of living,*
> *From hope and fear set free,*
> *We thank with brief thanksgiving*
> *Whatever gods may be*

---

*From "The Garden of Proserpine" (1866).

That no life lives forever.
That dead men rise up never;
That even the weariest river
Winds somewhere safe at sea.

Some people do not care to associate with pray-ing, preaching, singing, pious people on this earth, and they have no desire to spend all their time in the next life sitting in church or watching Chris-tian programs on television. Their view of heaven is not an appealing one.

Still others believe our lives should not be spent working for a heavenly reward. These people feel that being good on this earth is its own reward. We should live right simply because that's the right thing to do, not because we need the prom-ise of a future heaven to pay us for our goodness on earth. For these people the blessings that come from a life well lived are incentive enough.

Then there are those who think this world should engage one's full attention because life is a precious, present possession and one should be taking full advantage of all the opportunities it offers. Thinking about the next life takes our attention away from this life, they feel, and is therefore harmful.

Some feel, as did the rich man Jesus told about, "'Soul, thou hast much goods laid up for many years; take thine ease, eat, drink, and be merry'" (Luke 12:19). Such people happily live a life of self-indulgence. When they die, they leave as a heritage for their children the idea that living a good life on earth and leaving what we have for the next generation is reward enough.

In the book *Back to Methuselah* by George Bernard Shaw, Adam says, "If only I can be relieved of having to endure myself forever; if only the care of this terrible garden may pass on to some other gardener...if the rest and sleep that enable me to bear it from day to day, could grow after many days into eternal rest, and eternal sleep, then I could face my days, however long they may last. Only there must some end, some end! I am not strong enough to bear eternity."

Despite the views expressed in the preceding paragraphs, without the fact of eternal life the best of this present world is utterly lost. The belief that in the end the best is doomed to be lost is devastating because without immortality nothing can be eternally gained. Speaking of belief in eternity years ago, John Fiske, the well-known Harvard professor, said, "It is the supreme act of faith in the reasonableness of God's Work."

3

. . . .

DEATH IS "AWAKENING"

Some people feel we should give all our attention to the business of living in this world. Others give their time and thoughts to dreaming about the next world. However, many people concern themselves with both worlds. The greatest inspiration for giving selflessly to make things better on earth is a belief in a future "citizenship in heaven."

Life on earth can also inspire us to think of heaven because heaven is the place where all the aches and pains of this world are taken away, where there are no taxes to pay, where our homes, which are mansions, are free of debt and we have no bills to pay.

Remember how Jesus greeted his disciples after His Resurrection: "Jesus met them, saying, 'All hail'" (Matthew 28:9). The Greek word used here is *Xalpere*, which may be translated "Rejoice." The Lord is not only greeting His disciples, He is reporting. He had returned to earth from His Father's house.

You might wonder why we aren't given more specific descriptions of heaven. As a glorious sunrise or a piece of grand music defies description, likewise heaven is wordlessly magnificent.

If we really understood heaven, we would be most unhappy and unsatisfied with life on earth. We would rebel against our earthly limitations. If we saw heaven, we could not bear this earth. That's why heaven is forever. We cannot bear to leave it after we get there

Our present physical bodies are designed for our earthly life. We are not now prepared to view heaven. We trust God to supply all that we need to enable us to go into glorious life after death.

People have been observed as they die and for many it appears to be a beautiful and joyous experience. The words of William Cullen Bryant in "Thanatopsis" describe this transition from one life to the next:

Sustained and soothed
   by an unfaltering trust,
   approach the grave,
like one who wraps the drapery
   of his couch
About him, and lies down
   to pleasant dreams.

Death is not "sleep," but rather it is an "awakening." Percy Bysshe Shelley once wrote these words about his friend John Keats:

Peace, peace! he is not dead,
he does not sleep—
   He hath wakened
from the dream of life.

4

· · · · · · · · · · · ·

Heaven Is a Place

There is no greater promise in the Bible than the one expressed in John 3:16: "For God so loved the world, that he gave his only begotten Son, that whosoever believeth in him should not perish, but have everlasting life." *Belief in Jesus Christ is the only way to attain everlasting life.*

There is no substitute for belief in Jesus Christ. It is good to be kind to other people. It is wonderful to give gifts and be generous with money. It is right and proper to live a moral life. Nevertheless, no matter now good and moral someone is, if that person rejects Christ, he or she is doomed.

God does not have one plan of salvation for the rich and another for the poor. The same plan is for everyone. God did not put His plan up for a vote by the people. God did not ask if we would like it or not. God does not owe us salvation. God gives us the opportunity to accept it. We can take it or leave it.

Quoting the Psalmist, an old hymn says, "Whiter than snow—wash me and I shall be whiter than snow." Some people try to whitewash their sins, but God wants them washed white. When we repent and accept Christ, God not only gives us salvation, He also gives the gift of eternal life.

Heaven is not a state or a condition. *Heaven is a place.* "I go to prepare a place for you," promised Jesus. "In my Father's house are many mansions" (John 14:2). Salvation is not only the deliverance from our sins, it also means that we have a place to live throughout eternity.

What a great comfort to know that one of those mansions is reserved for us!

5

. . . .

Heavenly Treasures Are More Important

In the Sermon on the Mount, Jesus contrasted earthly treasures with heavenly rewards. While earthly goods afford temporary happiness, the rewards of heaven are eternal. Treasures on earth can be lost or stolen; treasures in heaven are safe forever. (See Matthew 6:19-21.)

This does not mean that we should refrain from storing possessions on this earth or saving money for later. We should use prudent foresight in regard to our needs. However, we should remember that heavenly treasures are more important.

Earthly treasures may be regarded as an important talent to be wisely used. Jesus said, "Ye cannot serve God and mammon" (Matthew 6:24). If your life is determined by the material things you can accumulate, you will sacrifice conscience and duty to God.

Certainly it is our privilege to better our circumstances. If we pursue wealth just to feed our pride, that wealth becomes a curse to the soul. Heavenly treasures are incorruptible and they secure and support immortality.

Treasures may be defined as provisions for the future. A bee or an ant has an instinct to provide for the future. Human beings have reason and experience to teach them. Because our physical lives require daily supplies, we should anticipate today the wants and needs of tomorrow. Heavenly treasures are resources for our immortal spirits. We need to consider both our lives that are now and our lives that are to come.

Jesus told us to "lay up for yourselves treasures in heaven" (Matthew 6:20). How do we "lay up" heavenly treasures? By believing in Christ as Lord and Savior, by expressing faith in right living, and by making God's cause on this earth our cause.

6

. . . .

Life Goes On Without the Body

S peaking to Timothy, his young friend and co-worker, the apostle Paul said, "Fight the good fight of faith, lay hold on eternal life" (1 Timothy 6:12). Paul really knew about the fight of faith. He had been through peril on land and sea; he had suffered both pain and disappointment. Earlier Paul had said to Timothy, "I have fought a good fight...I have kept the faith." Looking death in the face, Paul had once declared with confidence, "Henceforth there is laid up for me a crown of righteousness" (2 Timothy 4:7, 8).

At first Paul was confident of eternal life because he was a devout Pharisee and had been taught and believed there was eternal life. But Paul did not believe the reports that Jesus had risen from the grave. He believed the followers of Jesus were fanatics who should be eliminated and he watched with approval the stoning of Stephen.

Yet the faith of Stephen, as evidenced by his dying words, haunted Paul. "Behold, I see the heavens opened, and the Son of man standing on the right hand of God" (Acts 7:56). He thought about what Stephen had said he had seen. He wondered why those followers of Jesus believed their Lord was alive. Then on the road to Damascus one day Paul saw lights in the heavens and heard a voice saying to him, "Saul, Saul, why persecutest thou me?" Paul said, "Who art thou, Lord?" The Lord said, "I am Jesus whom thou persecutest. Arise, and go into the city and it shall be told thee what thou must do" (Acts 9:3-6).

Paul's experience on that fated road changed him forever. He never doubted the living Christ and he went out into the world, shouting to the people, "O death, where is thy sting? O grave, where is thy victory?...thanks be to God, which giveth us the victory through our Lord Jesus Christ" (1 Corinthians 15:55, 57).

Paul believed that life goes on even though the body has been buried in a grave. He clearly stated that "flesh and blood cannot inherit the kingdom of God" (1 Corinthians 15:50), but he explains the resurrection of the dead by stating, "It is sown a natural body; it is raised a spiritual body" (1 Corinthians 15:44). The body is just the dwelling place of the soul here on earth. Paul assures us, "For we know that if our earthly house of this tabernacle were dissolved, we have a building of God, an house not made with hands, eternal in the heavens" (2 Corinthians 5:1).

Sir Oliver Lodge put it this way, "Smashing an organ is not equivalent to killing the organist."

We assert our faith that life goes on without the body when we stand at the grave and repeat, "For as much as the departed has entered into life immortal, we therefore commit his body to the resting place, but his spirit we commend to God." (This is from the "Ritual for the Burial of the Dead," the United Methodist Church's *Book of Worship*.) These words recall how, on the cross, Jesus said, "Father, into thy hands I commend my spirit" (Luke 23:46).

As we fight the good fight of faith in this life. we do "lay hold on eternal life."

7

Three Fundamental Facts

J esus was truly the great comforter, as evidenced by these words: "Let not your heart be troubled....In my Father's house are many mansions" (John 14:1, 2). This is a statement each and every one of us can understand. *To die is to go and live in another home.* Most of us have had the experience of moving from one house to another. That is what death is. This is the answer to Job's question, "If a man die, shall he live again?" (Job 14:14).

Certainty of life after death is the crux of the Christian faith. There is no guessing, hesitation, dreaming, or hoping. There is one authoritative answer: "Because I live, ye shall live also" (John 14:19).

In the Bible God has given us three fundamental facts about life after death. First, we can be confident that *life follows death.* We can be absolutely certain that death is not the end. Death is not a sunset, but rather, a sunrise.

Jesus said heaven is a place, not a state of mind: "I go and prepare a place for you" (John 14:2). After death we are not disembodied spirits. Somewhere in God's wonderful creation there is a place where we can again be with those we have loved and lost for a while.

Second, *life after death is a state of perfect communion with God.* Often we feel frustrated. Our dreams don't come true. Our longings are not realized. John assures us, "And there shall be no night there [heaven]...for the Lord God giveth them light: and they shall reign for ever and ever" (Revelation 22:5). As we look forward to this place of joy and light, it is wonderful to know that heaven is a permanent residence.

Paul was a tent maker. He sewed the tents with his hands, and he erected them. No doubt many times he saw his tents blown down after a particularly severe storm. After a time the tents would become old and frayed. So it was with triumphant joy that Paul proclaimed, "For we know that if our earthly house of this tabernacle be destroyed, we have a building of God, an house not made with hands, eternal in the heavens" (2 Corinthians 5:1). John says of heaven, "And he shall go no more out" (Revelation 3:12). Heaven is a place where we unpack our bags and stay forever.

Third, *life is fuller and more complete in heaven.* On this earth we struggle for knowledge, as expressed in 1 Corinthians 13:12: "For now we see through a glass darkly." We struggle for purity, but we remain conscious of our impurities. We struggle for happiness, but it is only in heaven that we have hope of finding complete contentment.

As we think of eternal life, we say with Paul, "But thanks be to God, which giveth us the victory through our Lord Jesus Christ" (1 Corinthians 15:57).

When the enraged people of France put Louis XVI and his queen to death, a little boy was left who would have been Louis XVII if the monarchy had stood. The child was not put to death, but his captors did put him in prison. They surrounded him with vicious and vulgar men and told them to teach his mind to think vicious thoughts and his lips to say vulgar words. The story goes that as the lad grew and his evil companions would suggest some unsavory thought or word to him, he would stand at full height and say, "No, I will not think that. I cannot say that, for I was born to be a king."

As Christians we, too, are children of the King and are destined to be His heirs. With His help, we can resist the temptations of this world.

8

. . . .

God Is in Heaven

The Lord's Prayer begins, "Our Father, which art in Heaven...." Some people do not believe there is any heaven at all, but there are actually three heavens mentioned in the Bible.

When the Psalmist said, "The heavens declare the glory of God" (Psalm 19:1), the "heavens" refers to the air, the wind, and the clouds. It is what we see when we go outside and look up.

The same verse continues: "The firmament sheweth his handiwork." Here the Psalmist is referring to the moon, sun, and stars as being part of the firmament that is also referred to in Genesis 1:8: "And God called the firmament Heaven."

Some believe that the skies and space are the only heavens. But the heaven that Jesus referred to when He promised He was going there to prepare a place for His followers (John 14:2) is just as real as the skies and the stars. It is the heaven of heavens, the home of the blessed.

Those of us who believe in heaven expect to live there through eternity. In 1 Kings 8:30 the phrase "in heaven thy dwelling place" makes clear that God is not on earth but is not so far away that He cannot hear each of us when we pray. The pearly gates, jasper walls, and streets paved with gold are all fine and good, but the greatest thing about heaven is that God is there. "If my people, which are called by my name, shall humble themselves, and pray, and seek my face, and turn from their wicked ways; then will I hear from heaven, and will forgive their sin, and will heal their land" (2 Chronicles 7:14).

The great preacher Dwight L. Moody told about a little girl whose mother was sick. One of the neighbors took the child to care for her until the mother got well. But the mother died. When the neighbors took the child home after the funeral, she went into the living room to find her mother. Then she ran from room to room, asking, "Where is Mama?" When they explained that her mother was gone and would not be back, the little girl wanted to go back to the neighbor's house. She didn't want to be at home without Mama.

God's presence makes heaven what it is. And not only is God in heaven, but our loved ones who have died are also there. As Paul wrote, when we die we are "absent from the body...present with the Lord" (2 Corinthians 5:8). Heaven means to be reunited with our loved ones. In Luke 10:20 we read, "Rejoice, because your names are written in heaven."

Many of us have had a hotel clerk tell us there was no room reserved under our name. Such will never be the case in heaven: Our "rooms" are guaranteed by the Lord, if only we believe in His Son Jesus Christ.

9

. . . .

Certainty and Uncertainty Are Both Good

The experience of a continuing life is one every person on earth will have. Sooner or later, death is coming for all of us, but death is not the end of life.

Through the centuries many have testified that they have had communication with someone who has died. Many tell of hearing the voice of someone they knew, and some even say they have seen spirits.

Others take the logical approach and insist that our continued existence after death is fundamentally consistent with life on earth. On earth, in families, in churches, and in states, we struggle to bring ourselves together in love and peace. We more and more recognize our kinship with all human beings on earth. We work and pray for all people to love each other. After all our efforts for love to exist in the hearts of all people for all people, some find it inconsistent that death should end it all.

Then there are those who have lost loved ones through death yet continue to live with them as if they were alive. No one doubts the immortality of memory and influence. In a sense, people who have died are still alive as long as their memories remain. Our loved ones, in this way, continue to enrich and sweeten our lives long after their deaths.

Do we conclude that our dead are really dead and they only live in our imaginations?

There is an analogy in our Christian faith. We cannot demonstrate God's existence. However, we know that faith in a living God is reasonable and that faith unifies the lives we are living here. Likewise, we cannot demonstrate personal immortality. We do believe in eternal life and we trust the future for confirmation. In the meantime, our faith enables and adds glory to our lives here.

Still, some uncertainties about the continuation of our lives ought not to surprise or dismay us. Certainty and uncertainty are really not inconsistent. Uncertainties serve to discipline our character and deepen our lives.

For example, we sometimes wish we could see God as He is. But God is so great that in order for us to be able to see Him, He would have to become much, much less than He is. Our minds and eyes are not capable of fully beholding God. Really, it seems that God's love is too good to be true.

We prove our belief in God by living the lives such belief makes possible. As we accept our responsibilities for this day with cheerful courage, we increase our assurance of God and eternity. Living by faith, trusting our own visions, being inspired by those who have lived before us, we gain the certainty we need and an increased ability to communicate our faith to others.

10

. . . .

Believing Overcomes Fear

The Bible says, "It is appointed unto men once to die" (Hebrews 9:27). We know that death cannot be avoided. We do not know when but we do know each and every one of us will die.

So, accepting the fact of death, the inevitable question is, what comes next? That question is more urgent when it concerns the future of a dear loved one. It is unthinkable that our mother or father, brother or sister, or dear child should be forever lost.

Some people comfort themselves by saying that though the person has died, his or her influence will live on. Others say we live on in our children and in future generations. For a while we do live in these ways but that life fades rapidly and is usually forgotten after two or three generations.

Our assurance of life after death begins with our belief in the existence of God. If there is no God, we have no hope. Believing in God, we can say as Jesus said, "I lay down my life, that I might take it again" (John 10:17). *Therefore, each of us must now live the kind of life that gives evidence of eternity.* We must ask ourselves if our lives have eternal quality in them now, if within our lives there is the stuff of which heaven is made. Do we have compassion toward others? Do our lives confess that we have a citizenship in heaven?

Even though Jesus walked on earth, He made men and women think of heaven. We know that Jesus laid down His life, yet took it up again. People have a quality of the life eternal. We have something within us that lifts us upward. As we think of better things, we are better ourselves. In our minds we have a reverence for noble things that we cannot explain. Instinctively, we feel within ourselves a quality of the life eternal. As we seek to live the good life, we cannot think of ourselves as perishing.

Believing in immortality, we experience a victory over the fear of death.

11

· · · · · · · · · · · ·

Have You Had Your Good Friday?

The thief on the cross next to Jesus on Calvary gives hope and inspiration. In spite of the wrongs he had done, in spite of the fact he was almost at the end of his life, he believed there was still hope. He had not given up, as shown by his request, "Lord, remember me when thou comest into thy kingdom" (Luke 23:42). The thief, in short, is proof that it is never too late.

More important is the response of Jesus, considering that most significant moment in His life and the implications of that moment for all time. As He bled on the cross, He was suffering for all the sins of humankind. The world possesses no symbol that compares with the cross. Yet in this supreme moment Jesus took time to express loving concern for a dying thief.

Just two sentences, one from the thief and one from Jesus, give eternal hope: "Lord, remember me when thou comest into thy Kingdom" and

"Verily I say unto thee, today shalt thou be with me in paradise" (Luke 23:42, 43). Nothing more was said by either; all that was needed was said by each. The thief had reached out in repentance and faith, and Jesus offered acceptance in forgiving love and salvation.

Amid the jeering and howling mob a dying man asks another dying man to remember. Truly, here was an expression of faith and the reward of such trust.

Who was that dying thief? We do not know his name, where he lived, or anything about his family. Somehow he had gotten into trouble. We suppose he had a trial. He did not claim innocence; he made no excuses. Now he was paying for the wrongs of his life. He was at the end of his road. However, even at that dark moment, he knew there was a way out. He had faith there was One who could save him. There is humility in his prayer.

The thief did not ask for forgiveness. He did not mention salvation. He only had one word in mind: *remember*. He is expressing the deepest longing of the human heart. We all want to be remembered. We do not want to be forgotten.

How wonderful was Jesus' reply! There would be no long period of waiting. "Today," He said, "thou shalt be with me." Jesus was returning to His Father's house, and He was bringing with Him a new friend.

How encouraging for each of us! The first soul purchased by the blood of the King of Kings and the Lord of Lords is a poor thief and is a wonderful demonstration of God's loving mercy. We are reminded of Paul's words: "For by grace are ye saved through faith; and that not of yourselves: it is the gift of God" (Ephesians 2:8).

Today we believe that Jesus has spoken these same words to many others: to those who have felt guilt and shame; to those who have been disappointed in someone they loved; to those who have felt deep physical pain and suffering; and to whomever wanted to be remembered by Him. Good Friday did not happen just once. It comes again and again. The everlasting doors are open; heaven is the possession of anyone who looks to Jesus in the spirit of the dying thief.

If you have not experienced Jesus' saving grace, now is the time to say, "Lord, remember me."

12

. . . .

In Paradise With Him

Many have visited Oberammergau, Germany, where a Passion play is presented every ten years. On a hill high above the village stands a cross, the focal point of the entire area.

High above all of human history stands a cross on a hill called Calvary, the cross of Christ. For Christians this rough-hewn cross is the focal point of human history, the greatest event since the creation.

For two thousand years the power of the cross has not diminished. As we study the faces surrounding the cross, we realize they are people like us. In humility, we realize we are like those who crucified Him.

As we gaze at the cross, we realize we are looking into one of God's mirrors, and we see ourselves through God's eyes. We see the person we are, and we realize how wide the gulf is between the person we see and the person God wants us to be.

Today depictions of the cross are works of art, but there was no beauty in the cross that stood on Calvary. Crucifixion was the most horrible death known in Jesus' time. In fact, the Romans never inflicted crucifixion on any citizen of the Roman Empire.

But the crucifixion of Christ is not just an event of the distant past; it is also an event of this present moment. A well-known hymn asks the question, "Were you there when they crucified my Lord?" The answer is yes: We, too, are standing under the cross.

As Jesus neared death, He called out, "Father, forgive them; for they know not what they do" (Luke 23:34). The cross teaches us our need for forgiveness and salvation. The wonder and reality of God's forgiveness and infinite love come directly from the cross of Jesus.

Furthermore, the cross reveals God's purpose: "God was in Christ, reconciling the world unto himself" (2 Corinthians 5:19). The depth and power of God's love is illuminated through the cross: "For God so loved the world, that he gave his only begotten Son" (John 3:16); "And I, if I be lifted up from the earth, will draw all men unto me" (John 12:32).

We all have the same opportunity as the thief on the cross. We can all be on the other side of death—in paradise—with Him.

13

. . . .

Calvary and Easter Go Together

In the little book of Jude we read, "Keep yourselves in the love of God, looking for the mercy of our Lord Jesus Christ unto eternal life" (Jude 1:21). Every person, at least half-consciously, knows that death is the final stage of life on this earth.

But consider this: Calvary and Easter go together. If Christ had not risen, death would have handed Him a failure. As far as people are concerned, forgiveness and eternal life go hand in hand. If eternal life were not real, then forgiveness would be like the last meal before the electric chair. But when death becomes real in our minds and hearts, we remember the words of the Philippian jailor to Paul and Silas: "Sirs, what must I do to be saved?" (Acts 16:30).

We want to believe that death, as birth, is a normal and natural event. Everyone knows birth is the beginning of life, and no one wants to accept the idea that death is final. We all reach out in hope for another world. When a loved one dies, we cannot help thinking about the next world. We recognize our own physical frailties and are driven to wonder what comes next.

The Bible tells us, "The last enemy that shall be destroyed is death" (1 Corinthians 15:26). Unless there is life beyond death, where is the victory in destroying death? Faith in the existence of the next world may not be constant, and at times there may be doubts, but we continue to believe.

Napoleon once asked how long a portrait someone had painted would last. He was told that eight hundred years would be the limit. He responded, "Such a poor immortality! I want to live not for eight hundred years, nor for eighty times eight hundred, but forever!"

More than any other person or event, Jesus Christ, through His teachings, His death, and His Resurrection, meets the faith and hopes of humanity for eternal life. Life and immortality both become real through the Gospel of Jesus Christ.

Jesus gave humanity forgiveness and confidence. Because of Him, we know that beyond the darkness of death, there is sunshine.

Paul tells us, "And if Christ be not risen, then is our preaching in vain, and your faith is also vain" (1 Corinthians 15:14). He also wrote, "And that he was seen of Cephas, then of the twelve: after that, he was seen of above five hundred brethren at once; of whom the greater part remain unto this present, but some are fallen asleep" (1 Corinthians 15:5, 6).

The Bible says it clearly, carefully, and confidently.

This is the foundation of the Christian church. Without the Resurrection, faith in Christ would have died and the church would not exist. The early church took as its foundation the words in Job 19:25, "For I know that my Redeemer liveth, and that he shall stand at the latter day upon the earth."

The proof of Christ's Resurrection is His presence. Christians believe in bringing heaven to earth. They don't believe we must live one world at a time; they know that even on earth we can experience some of the wonderful world to come through Christ's presence.

John wrote, "And I heard a voice from heaven...I heard the voice of harpers harping with their harps" (Revelation 14:2). All the conflicts of this world—the hatred, fear, and resentment—are resolved in the musical harmony of heaven.

14

. . . .

Easter Is Not a Spring Festival

For many Easter is a spring festival, a time to see the leaves coming out on the trees, to rejoice in the warming weather, to admire the blooming flowers, and to plant seeds in our gardens. But all these reactions or events are not Easter. And while we're on the subject, Easter is not bunny rabbits, candy eggs, or bright new clothes either.

Easter is the time to sing "Christ the Lord is risen today, Alleluia," "Up from the grave, He arose, with a mighty triumph o'er His foes," and "He lives, He lives, Christ Jesus lives today," among other Easter hymns.

We believe that in the tomb owned by Joseph of Aramathea the soul of Jesus returned to His dead body. After an angel rolled away the stone that sealed the tomb, Jesus came out and walked into the garden. The Resurrection had occurred! The fact of the empty tomb has never been denied.

Jesus made the glorious promise to His disciples in that day and to those who believe in Him now: "Because I live, ye shall live also" (John 14:19). There is life beyond the grave!

Our hearts are stirred when we remember songs such as the following:*

> *Shall we gather at the river,*
> *Where bright angel feet have trod;*
> *With its crystal tide forever*
> *Flowing by the throne of God?*
>
> *Ere we reach the shining river,*
> *Lay we ev'ry burden down;*
> *Grace our spirits will deliver,*
> *And provide a robe and crown.*
>
> *Soon we'll reach the shining river,*
> *Soon our pilgrimage will cease;*
> *Soon our happy hearts will quiver*
> *With the melody of peace.*

---

*From "Shall We Gather at the River?" by Robert Lowry.

Yes, we'll gather at the river,
The beautiful, the beautiful river.
Gather with the saints at the river
That flows by the throne of God.

The tragedy of many people today is they are not on a pilgrimage anywhere. As they look into the beyond, they see no place to go. They forget they have souls. The death of a Christian does not mean that person's life like a flame has been extinguished. Rather, that person, *as a Christian*, has gone to be with the Lord eternally.

Speaking of life through a character in *Macbeth*, William Shakespeare wrote:

It is a tale told
By an idiot, full of sound and fury
Signifying nothing.

Those of us who love the Lord don't share this dark and despairing view. Meaning and happiness in this life are found in living the way God desires. Still, we feel deep longings that are never satisfied, aspirations for a different life. We know that there will be another life after this one, a life in God's presence

15

. . . .

Jesus' Four Contacts with Death

Through the centuries people have sought either a promise or a revelation upon which they can establish their hope and belief in life after death. Writing to Timothy, Paul said that Jesus Christ "hath abolished death, and hath brought life and immortality to light through the gospel" (2 Timothy 1:10).

Jesus brought back to this life three people who had died: the widow's son at Nain, the daughter of Jairus, and Lazarus. Jesus Himself arose from the dead.

If human beings only returned to dust when they died, Jesus' death on the cross would be a great tragedy. But because God's love for us is so overwhelming, the cross proclaims victoriously the infinite worth of humans and, therefore, their immortality. Through the cross, those who profess belief in Jesus Christ are assured of "glory and honour and immortality, eternal life" (Romans 2:7).

The widow of Nain lost her only son. He was a young man on the threshold of adult life when he died. As she and her friends and neighbors were on the way to the cemetery, Jesus and His disciples met them. Then we read, "And when the Lord saw her, he had compassion on her, and said unto her, 'Weep not.' And he came and touched the bier: and they that bare him stood still. And he said, 'Young man, I say unto thee, Arise.' And he that was dead sat up, and began to speak. And he delivered him to his mother" (Luke 7:13-15).

Jesus had another contact with the dead when Jairus asked Him to come to his house to heal his daughter. However, the daughter died before Jesus could come. Jesus said, "Fear not; believe only, and she shall be made whole." When they went into the house, Jesus said, "Weep not. She is not dead, but sleepeth." Then, "They all laughed him to scorn, knowing that she was dead." Jesus said, "Maid, arise." She immediately got up and Jesus commanded them to give her meat. The parents were astonished. This story is told in Luke 8:41-56 and in Mark 5:22-43.

The third experience occurred with Jesus' friend Lazarus. This experience is different from the others because Jesus deliberately let Lazarus die. Word was sent to Jesus that "He whom thou lovest is sick." Instead of hurrying to see Lazarus, Jesus waited two days. Then Jesus said to His disciples, "Let us go into Judea again...Our friend Lazarus sleepeth, but I go, that I awake him out of sleep." The disciples thought he was speaking of normal sleep, but Jesus knew Lazarus was dead.

When they arrived they discovered Lazarus had been buried four days earlier. Martha went out to meet Jesus and said, "If thou hadst been here, my brother had not died." Jesus said, "Thy brother shall rise again." Martha replied, "I know he shall rise in the resurrection at the last day."

Then Jesus made a glorious statement: "I am the resurrection, and the life: he that believeth in me, though he were dead, yet shall he live: and whosoever liveth and believeth in me shall never die."

When Jesus arrived at the grave, "He cried with a loud voice, 'Lazarus, come forth,' and Lazarus came forth out of the grave." (This story is from John 11:1-44.)

Fourth, of course, Jesus experienced His own death. His farewell words are the most precious in the Bible about the future life. John 14 is where these words are recorded: "I go to prepare a place for you...I am the way, the truth and the life...Peace I leave with you, my peace I give unto you...Let not your heart be troubled, neither let it be afraid."

Jesus is the Resurrection and the life for two reasons. First, we have life because of our redemption through His victory over death. Second, as Paul said, "Now is Christ risen from the dead, and become the firstfruits of them that slept" (1 Corinthians 15:20). Jesus' words again come to mind: "In my Father's house are many mansions"

(John 14:2). We joyfully sing John Newton's lyrics:

> *When we've been there ten thousand years,*
> *Bright shining as the sun,*
> *We've no less days to sing God's praise*
> *Than when we first begun.*

16

. . . .

To Live Is Christ, To Die Is Gain

Paul did not see the cross of Christ on Calvary. Yet as he was facing his own death he declared, "For me to live is Christ, and to die is gain" (Philippians 1:21).

Paul was in a prison cell, soon to stand trial before Nero, and there was a chance he would be set free. Writing to his friends, he said, "I thank my God upon every remembrance of you" (Philippians 1:3).

The thought of death brings to mind memories of all those we love. We do not want to be separated from them. This is one of the sadder things, if not the saddest thing about death.

To his loved ones Paul wrote, "For God is my record, how greatly I long after you" (Philippians 1:8). We should long after those we love. We do not want them to leave.

Instead of being set free, Paul knew he might be facing death. For him, the possibility of death was not far in the future. Yet Paul did not think of death with fear and trembling. He did not refuse to face the fact of death, as many people today. He knew he could not eliminate death by refusing to consider it.

Some people say they do not care what comes after death. They certainly are not thinking of their loved ones. At the funeral of your mother or father, your brother or sister, your husband or wife, your son or daughter, you care very much what comes after death. Sooner or later every person will ask the question Job asked, "If a man die, shall he live again?" (Job 14:14)

None of us can say it does not matter whether one we love ends up as a handful of dirt or consciously alive in the Father's house.

So Paul is not afraid. He can face either life here or in the hereafter. Paul could say "to die is gain" because of the values he possessed on this earth. Some people feel to live is money or fame, comfort or pleasure, and so on. Hear Paul's words again: "For me to live is Christ." That made the difference.

At this moment Paul was thinking of his experience on the road to Damascus when he was confronted by Christ. "Lord, what wilt thou have me do?" (Acts 4:6). He called Jesus, Lord.

To find God through Christ is to find life eternal, and there is no other way. Paul believed that being with Christ here he would continue to live with Him through eternity.

Not only did Paul believe that in eternity he would have a closer fellowship with Christ, he also believed he would have fellowship with those who had died before him. Likewise may be our faith. We look forward to seeing our loved ones who have gone on before us. Heaven will be home because the same characteristics that make home here will make it home in the next life. Home is where we live with our loved ones.

If we could go back to the home where we grew up, we would find it a lonely place. Our loved ones are not there. Also, many of us can remember the pain or sorrow some of our loved ones felt on this earth. In the next life pain and sorrow do not exist.

We do not resent the rest and reward of our loved ones who have died. We know that our pain, sorrow, and disappointments will one day be no more. Even though we have so much to live for on this earth, there is even more to live for in the next life. Death does not cheat a person out of life; death enriches life.

Remember: "For me to live is Christ, and to die is gain."

17

· · · · · · · · · · · ·

Death Is Our Harvest Time

D eath is the close of the seed time of life and the beginning of life's harvest. Our dreams, our hopes, our aspirations, and our desires cannot be fulfilled on this earth. In the life to come, hope is turned into fruition, and aspiration into attainment.

We can be sure that the God who planted yearnings in our hearts prepared for those yearnings to be satisfied. On this earth we are born with a thirst for water, and indeed water flows all around us. Our lungs crave oxygen, and on this earth the supply of air is unlimited.

We have a longing in our hearts to live, and God has prepared a place for us where we will never die. We take comfort and inspiration in the words of Jesus, "Let not your heart be troubled: ye believe in God, believe also in me. In my Father's house are many mansions: if it were not so, I would have told you. I go to prepare a place for you" (John 14:1, 2).

The butterfly would not exist if the worm had not gone through a transformation after which it—the worm—ceased to exist. Death is a passing through the transformation process. Our body dies, but then we, too, have wings. *Death is a birth into another life.* Birth and death are really one and the same thing: We are born into this world and we are born out of this world.

There is a Persian proverb that says, "When a man is born, he begins to die; when he dies, he begins to live."

Speaking to the seventy, Jesus said, "Rejoice because your names are written in heaven" (Luke 10:20). Likewise, as Christians, each and every one of us can rejoice.

Many people at some period in their lives experience within themselves a consciousness of the eternal, also referred to as a "cosmic consciousness." This feeling gives one inspiration and power

In his life and teachings, Jesus demonstrated

proofs of immortality. His actual mastery over death caused Paul to write, "O death, where is thy sting? O grave, where is thy victory? ...Thanks be to God, which giveth us the victory through our Lord Jesus Christ" (1 Corinthians 15:55,57).

18

· · · · · · · · · · · ·

Life's Graduation

The Bible tells us that death is not the end of life but rather, the doorway into a life where all our needs are met and all sorrows ended. "They shall hunger no more, neither thirst any more...and God shall wipe away all tears from their eyes" (Revelation 7:16,17).

In the next life our worries will be over: no debts, nothing to be afraid of, no health problems, and no unhappy concerns about our family or friends.

Many have reported seeing happiness spring up in people as they come to the end of life's road. Many believe one gets a quick look into the next life as one is leaving this one, and that what they see is good, real good. What we have accumulated on this earth, we happily leave to others. What we receive in the next life is much, much better.

We think of the separation from this life as death, and we think of death as the end. Really, death is the gateway into eternity where the rewards never cease. Death is life's graduation. Death is the transference from the physical to the spiritual plane.

There's wisdom to be found in a Chinese funeral custom. While westerners tend to wear black or dark colors to funerals to express sorrow, the Chinese custom has been the opposite. White is worn to convey joy at the moving of loved ones from this world to the next.

Be assured God expects us to live in the here and now. Still there comes a time when many who have reached the winter of life look longingly toward the next, wanting to be with the Lord and loved ones who have gone before, wanting to escape the trials and tribulations they are facing. Having lived a full and busy life, they are tired and want to rest.

God arranged for the loving hands of a mother to be waiting to receive a baby when it is born into this world. Likewise, we can be assured there will be no fear as we enter the next life. There will be a welcome for us into that beautiful land.

19

. . . .

Not "Future" Life

There is a vast difference between the terms "life after death" and "future life." Future life is something we can have while still living here and that will continue and come to full fruition only in the future. Life after death implies a life we wait for until the end of life on earth.

Faith in life after death is faith in a life that is fuller and better than our present existence. The incompleteness of life on earth is erased. This faith enables us to "make sense" of life in the present. However, it is the character and nature of God, as revealed through Jesus Christ, rather than the character and nature of man, that provides the basis of an assured faith in personal life after death.

The depth of one's faith in life after death is based on the quality of his or her fellowship with God. God's love is forever. He calls us into fellowship with Himself and He will never abandon us. Father-love is eternal. The Psalmist said, "Thou wilt shew me the path of life: in thy presence is fulness of joy; at thy right hand there are pleasures for evermore" (Psalm 16:11).

God is not only just and righteous but also fatherly and loving. Jesus said, "He is not the God of the dead, but the God of the living" (Mark 12:27). Fellowship with God is not interrupted or ended by death. We remember the very last recorded words of Jesus before His death on the cross: "Father, into thy hands I commend my spirit" (Luke 23:46).

Then came the ultimate assurance of life after death: the Resurrection. In the Resurrection of Jesus we see the power and love of the Heavenly Father, proof that God will not suffer fellowship with Him to be destroyed. God is able to triumph over death. As Paul put it, the death and Resurrection of Christ "hath brought life and immortality to light" (2 Timothy 1:10).

20

. . . .

Where You Have Been
Is Not As Important
As Where You Are Going

Sometimes people feel life is trivial because they fail to think of earthly life in connection with eternity. When we think of ourselves as a kind of animal, yet with a mind and soul, despair often results. If we believe we might be cut down like a beast in the field, with nothing else ahead, God appears a cruel jester. The widely held belief that death ends all may help to explain why there is so much cynicism today.

The more we focus on eternity, the more loyal we are in our faith. The more sensitive we are to God, the less likely we are to believe that we are just animals to be dumped into the pit of death. As we mature in our Christian faith, we become convinced that our dreams, hopes, impulses, and love will live on in eternity.

If we let it, eternity can profoundly influence our lives. Under that influence, we are gentler when provoked, more honest when tempted, and more resolute and determined as we face the trials of life.

More important, eternity in our minds increases our awareness of the joys that are the best. *We are more apt to feel content.* Eternity makes us realize that the bright experiences in life are like stars that keep shining through the storms.

We know that many of the joys or goals of this life are not truly fulfilling. Eating to satisfy our fleshly desires, seeking prestige among other people, and possessing great sums of money often result in poor physical and mental health and personal discord. The bottom line is this: If this earthly life is all there is, we tend to lose our interest in living.

Be assured that just as an hour is only part of a day, so life on earth is only part of eternity. The important part of humankind is not the long, long years of the pact that goes back to creation. The important years are those that lead into the future. Where you have been is not as important as where you are going.

21

. . . .

You Won't Waste Your Time in the Grave

J esus said, "And this is life eternal, that they may know thee, the only true God" (John 17:3). The assurance of God is the assurance of heaven. Without God, we cannot even imagine heaven.

If we muff our opportunity to know and fellowship with God, that is hell.

Paul said to Timothy, "Fight the good fight of faith, lay hold on eternal life" (1 Timothy 6:12). He is saying one does not need to die to experience eternal life. *The emphasis is on the present moment.*

Some people have the idea that when we die, we go into a long sleep in the grave. Then, when the world comes to an end, all people will be resurrected and come before the judgment seat of God. After the judgment we will enter heaven or hell.

Such a view does violence to both the character of God and the teachings of Jesus. In our very limited human life, none of us could ever *earn* eternal punishment or eternal joy. The brief life on earth is not the whole life. Life on this earth is only the beginning. Jesus said, "The kingdom of heaven is like to a grain of mustard seed" (Matthew 13:31). Just as a seed is the beginning of growth, so this life is the beginning but not the end. We continue living the moment our spirits are released from our bodies.

Jesus said, "I am the God of Abraham, and the God of Isaac, and the God of Jacob. God is not the God of the dead, but of the living" (Matthew 22:32). Abraham, Isaac, and Jacob are not in some grave, waiting for resurrection. They are living now. In fact, Jesus talked with Moses and Elijah on the Mount of Transfiguration (Matthew 17:2).

The number of years someone has lived does not qualify them for eternal life. When we feel that someone dies too young, we miss the point. Methuselah lived longer than anyone else, but he did not accomplish much. The Bible gives his life story in one verse: "And all the days of Methuselah were nine hundred sixty and nine years, and he died" (Genesis 5:27). He did not accomplish anything in all his years worth reporting.

The measure of a life—the worth of a person—requires a different scale. Remember: Realize the present moment. Many people live in the future in their younger years and in the past in their older years. As we face life in the here and now, and as we feel new strength and guidance in living today, we become more and more conscious of the presence of God and more alive to eternity.

One of the most comforting stories is recorded in the eleventh chapter of John. The friend of Jesus, Lazarus, has died. Lazarus had two sisters, Mary and Martha, and we read how many of the Jews came to these women to comfort them concerning their brother. Friends should comfort friends when a loved one has died.

We know what happened next. When Martha heard that Jesus was coming, she went and confronted Him: "If thou hadst been here, my brother had not died" (John 11:21). Often, as people experience sorrow, they feel God has deserted them.

Jesus assured Martha that her brother would rise again. But that was not comforting to Martha. She said, "I know that he shall rise again in the resurrection at the last day" (John 11:24).

Then we read, "Jesus said unto her, 'I am the resurrection, and the life: he that believeth in me, though he were dead, yet shall he live: and whosoever liveth and believeth in me shall never die'' (John 11:25, 26).

God did not plan for us to waste our time in a grave.

22

. . . .

God Is Not Nowhere...
He Is Now Here

O ur universe consists of two worlds: the one we now live in and the one we will live in after death. Birth is the beginning of a life. Death is the continuation of life. One is the same person after death.

Through the years it has been taught that life on earth is the vestibule of the next life. We are to prepare ourselves in the vestibule before we enter the palace. Much has been written explaining the mysteries of life in the next world. In poetry, song, and story, we hear about the life to come.

However, we know for sure only one thing about the next life: We know nothing.

If we believe, as stated in the Bible, "For my thoughts are not your thoughts, neither are your ways, my ways, saith the Lord" (Isaiah 55:8), we shouldn't expect to know about the next life. Our small brains cannot grasp infinity. "The thunder of his power who can understand?" (Job 26:14)

Belief in the next world essentially means belief in the actuality of God. We can be like the atheist who said, "God is nowhere," or the believer who said, "God is now here."

At the burning bush God said to Moses, "Put off thy shoes from off thy feet, for the place whereon thou standest is holy ground" (Exodus 3:5). Similarly, the earth on which we stand should impress us with the fact of God's existence. The earth is holy.

On earth we learn to obey the requirements of good health: clean air, good food and drink, and plenty of sleep. We respect the laws of water and fire, of falling and flying. As mortals we long for immortality. As the Psalmist wrote, "I shall not die, but live, and declare the works of the Lord" (Psalm 118:17).

We confess we know nothing, but we sense the world where we will live after death even though we see it through a window deeply stained. Without positive proof or certain evidence, we do possess persuasive intimations.

On this earth people are constantly seeking beauty, truth, and peace. It is hard to believe that God would create a Moses or an Elijah and then throw them out to perish, never to be used again. It is also hard to believe God would throw out any of His children, even you or me.

23

· · · · · · · · · · · ·

The Three Anxieties of Life

P eople feel three major anxieties. The first concerns identity. We want to be recognized, to have people say, "I am glad to see you." Nobody wants to be a nobody. We like to see our names in print. Most of us will not become world renowned, but we do want to have our own identity. Therefore it is inspiring to believe that in the sight of God each one of us counts.

The second anxiety is we want to enjoy living. Just to be alive is not enough. We want some excitement and challenges. One who is bored becomes boring. Boredom is deadening. Our lives need a purpose in order to have meaning and joy.

The third anxiety is security. We want to feel safe. When we go to bed at night, or when we walk down the street, we do not want to feel we are in danger. We want reasonable assurance that we will have enough of the material things of life to meet our needs. We want to know that medical science can take care of our physical ills. We want to feel secure in the love of family and friends.

More important than these anxieties of life is the anxiety about death. We may want to push the thought from our minds, but we know we will die. Some ask, "If we must die, what is the purpose of life?"

As they faced death long ago, the response of the Epicureans was to "eat, drink, and be merry for tomorrow we die." Some would agree with those who say, "If there is no life after death, if the grave is the end, then why not kick up our heels and make the most of it?"

One Native American concept of death involved a trip to the happy hunting grounds. The assurance of eternal hunting was the one most wanted. To be sure, death should be regarded as a vital dimension of life.

If there were no death and life on this earth were forever, many of the joys of life would not be experienced. Since the expulsion of Adam and

Eve from the Garden of Eden, everything in nature lives and dies. Realizing that we live only a relatively short time lends zest to living. Death puts a value on living. We do not think of life ending in old age, but moving into an eternal life. It would be terrible to face living forever with all the infirmities of old age. If we live long enough, we can count on our eyesight and hearing deteriorating, our memory failing, and our bodies becoming weaker and weaker. Death promises a sure escape. Without death, there could never be a satisfying view of life.

How then should we face death? Not by shallow living, eating, drinking, and being merry. Not by refusing to be near the sick and ignoring the fact of dying. Not by being paralyzed by fear so that we cannot live while we are living.

Instead, we should see death as a challenge that makes this life more meaningful, develops our potential, and stirs our enthusiasm. Death brings relief after our bodies are spent. Death assures us we need not fear when "our tale is told."

What happens after death? We can be sure that God knows what is best for us. God created life and we can trust Him to continue His creating love for us in the next life. We believe in a God who has a plan for everything.

As he interceded for the evil cities of Sodom and Gomorrah, Abraham said, "Shall not the Judge of all the earth do right?" (Genesis 18:25). This is our faith.

24

. . . .

When the Night Is Darkest

The singing of the nightingale has been said to sound sweetest when the night is darkest. For most of us, death—our own or that of a dear loved one—is the darkest night because it seems so final. When death strikes one near to us, a black shadow seems to be cast across our lives.

As we go along in life all of us experience illness, disappointments, and hurts. Most of us keep moving through the pain and anguish, but the death of a loved one is different. Death is hard to accept.

The Psalmist said, "Yea, though I walk through the valley of the shadow of death" (Psalm 23:4). As David the shepherd led his sheep through that valley, he most likely could see and hear prowling beasts, marauding thieves, and hard-riding robbers. The valley was constantly dangerous for the shepherd. The same is true for each of us. As we, our families, and our friends go through life, we face constant threats. Death can come at the most unexpected moments, and neither wealth nor power can insulate us against its threat. We can exercise caution, call upon the services of physicians, and live according to the rules of health, but death's shadow still hangs over life.

As the shepherd walked "through the valley," he had the support of his faith that God was with him. That assurance overcame his panic. He walked with courage and calmness because he trusted in the presence of God.

The glory of our own faith is that it enables us to believe that no matter how dark the shadows, we can keep going. Even though the path of our lives leads us through the experience of death, eventually we come out of the valley into open fields and eternal life.

Sometimes we complain that we suffer as much or more than those who have no faith in God. Sometimes we think unrighteous people have more fun and joy in life than we do. Sometimes we feel the unrighteous prosper more, have fewer loads to bear, and are less encumbered by moral restraints. However, our Christian faith gives us great advantages. We have help in the time of distress that the ungodly do not have. The Christian does not need to face life trembling with fear. We can say with the Psalmist, "I will fear no evil, for thou art with me."

Being a passenger in an airplane during rough weather is not a pleasant experience. The bouncing and sudden drops can be cause for concern. But we believe the pilot is capable and the plane sturdy enough to go through the weather safely. Imagine being in the midst of a storm without a pilot! You would feel helpless and hopeless. Likewise in life, when trouble comes, those without faith feel no ministering Presence near them. They hear no reassuring call. They have no triumphant hope.

Faith in God is not a special gift for a few, like the talent for music or for art. *Anyone who really desires faith can be a spiritual success.* Just as we become physically strong through lifting weights, so we become spiritually mature through exercising faith. We have to exercise our spiritual faculties.

Faith is the one thing we need when we face the fact of death. Courage comes as we, like the shepherd in the twenty-third Psalm, put our trust in God.

25

. . . .

Do Not Be Afraid

One of the greatest statements made on this earth was one the angel made after Christ's Resurrection: "Fear not ye:...He is not here: for he is risen" (Matthew 28:5, 6).

At dawn the day after Jesus was buried, Mary Magdalene and the other Mary came to visit His sepulchre. An angel had already descended from heaven and rolled back the stone from the tomb. The angel said to the women, "Come see the place where the Lord lay." Then the angel told them to go tell the disciples. (Matthew 28:1-8)

"Fear not ye." To use a big word, the angel was advising the women to be *indomitable*. If we are indomitable, we can be victorious, *we cannot be defeated*. In other words, if we are Christians, the sorrows, disappointments, frustrations, and defeats of life can be overcome. "He is risen!" Knowing that to be true, we do not need to be afraid.

As we place our faith in a Christ who overcame death, we feel a sense of greatness. In spite
of what happens, through Jesus Christ we can
overcome. The physical hurts and defeats cannot
destroy us mentally and spiritually. When we
reach the place where we have no fear of life and
no fear of death, we have won the greatest of all
possible victories.

Many people fear the insecurities of this world:
sickness, lack of money, loss of loved ones, natural disasters. But when we meditate on how Christ
was crucified and then resurrected, and when we
commit our lives to Him, we are not afraid. Christian indomitability is truly a great possession.

No normal person wants to die. We enjoy our
lives on this earth. In spite of imperfections, this
is a lovely world. We do not want to leave it. This
is the only life we know.

As Christians, we do not believe God would
move us from this world into a place of ugliness.
We cannot believe that the God who "so loved
the world" would ever become cruel. We cannot

believe that the God of creation would ever change into a God of death and destruction. When we see the sun rise every morning, we know God is an orderly God. We cannot believe He would ever become disorderly. We have to believe that death, when it finally comes, will be another expression of God's love, beauty, and planning.

26

. . . .

Heaven Is Not a Reward
for Good Behavior

J esus taught us how to live happy and con- structive lives here on this earth. Also, He taught us that our lives here are linked with eternity and with God. Life in heaven is a continuance of life on earth. Jesus said, "I am come that they might have life, and that they might have it more abundantly" (John 10:10). He also said, "My sheep hear my voice...and I give unto them eternal life; and they shall never perish" (John 10:27, 28). Heaven is a gift to humankind, not a reward for being good.

Birth is not a tragedy but a triumph; death is likewise. We have a tendency to think of death as a gloomy, defeating experience, a dark, lonely valley where there is no sun.

Think of a child who lives in a home with a loving family. One day that child leaves home to go to college. To leave home is indeed a traumatic experience. On the other hand, it would be worse if that child could never leave home and go out into a larger world. Likewise, death is not easy to face, but to be condemned to live forever on this earth would be worse. Leaving this earth we go into a much larger life, an eternal life with Jesus Christ.

After we receive Christ into our lives, we develop qualities that Paul listed in Galatians 5:22, 23: "But the fruit of the Spirit is love, joy, peace, longsuffering, gentleness, goodness, faith, meekness, temperance." In heaven those qualities continue to develop in an existence that is timeless and immeasurable. Anyone who has difficulty accepting the fact of the next life should remember the words of the prophet, "Have faith in God" (Isaiah 11:22).

Through Christ there is rapprochement—a restoring of harmony—between the imperfections of the human person and the perfect goodness of God. Through Jesus Christ, people can live naturally as sons and daughters of God.

27

. . . .

God Would Not Close the Door

If we believe in God, we must believe in eternal life. Some people believe in eternal life because of their own feelings of importance; they cannot imagine not existing. However, it is not a person's importance, but *God's importance* that really counts. We cannot imagine a God who would create this universe and then just throw it away.

When he died Franz Schubert had yet to complete his later named "Unfinished Symphony." Without eternity, human life is unfinished. The more we achieve in this life, the more we see there is to achieve. Life on this earth is never finished but simply continues into the next life. As we grow older, life becomes more important and our desire to continue life grows stronger.

Paul said, "But as it is written, Eye hath not seen, nor ear heard, neither have entered into the heart of man, the things which God hath prepared for them that love him" (1 Corinthians 2:9). However, in order to see, hear, and experience what God has prepared, "this mortal must put on immortality" (1 Corinthians 15:53). Just as a baby in the womb cannot experience this world, so we cannot experience the next until we are born into it.

Without eternity the final symbol of every life is simply a closed door. Christians who believe in the God who "so loved the world that he gave his only begotten Son" (John 3:16) cannot believe that He will close the door in their faces.

What would life on this earth be like if no one believed in eternal life? The spiritual climate would be drastically different and much of life's meaning would be lost. If life were merely mortal, then many people would not feel it is worth living. Most of us would agree with Edna St. Vincent Millay: "I am not resigned to the shutting away of loving hearts in the hard ground."*

We have faith in the existence of eternal life

---

*From "Dirge without Music" (1928).

not just because we want to live, but more because of our loved ones who have died. How can
any person experience the death of a parent,
spouse, or child and feel it does not matter
whether or not there is a life after this one? We
want our loved ones to keep living. We want to
see and be with them again.

Alfred, Lord Tennyson once penned these
words:*

> *Thou modest man, he knows not why*
> *He thinks he was not made to die,*
> *And thou has made him: thou art just.*

The faith we have in the next life makes our
lives here meaningful. Johann von Goethe said,
"These are dead even for this life who hope for
no other."

We know that ahead the door is open. That is
really all we need to know.

---

*From "In Memoriam" (1850).

28

. . . .

Not Eternal Rest...Eternal Life

T hose of us who must contend with living in or near large metropolitan areas surely have a concept of heaven: no cars, no traffic, no pollution!

We often think we would like to have a complete description of our future life in heaven. The fact that the Bible says so little about what heaven is like has troubled some Christians.

One problem is that our language is mostly limited to our own experiences. For example, how would you describe the colors of the rainbow to a person who was born blind? Just try one color, blue, for example. What would you say that would cause a blind person to see the color blue in his or her mind? One dictionary defines blue this way: "Blue, a color whose hue is that of the clear sky or that of the portion of the color spectrum lying between green and violet." Hearing that definition would not help at all. One has to see blue in order to know what it is like.

Similarly, having lived only on this earth, we cannot imagine what heaven will be like. The main thing we need to know about heaven, however, is that immediately upon arrival we are in the presence of Christ. "Today shalt thou be with me in paradise," Jesus said to the man dying by his side (Luke 23:43). In the Phillips translation, the same verse reads, "I tell you truly, this very day you will be with me in paradise."

Here we have the assurance that the continuity of life is not interrupted by death. There is no long wait in some suspended state, whether the grave or some other place. Life...death...God's presence...they immediately follow each other.

Note that Jesus used the word "paradise," which means beauty and delight, to convey a place of supreme magnificence. We think of the words of Jesus, "In my Father's house are many mansions," (John 14:2), and we see in our minds those stately mansions.

Paradise is used only three times in the Bible:

the preceding reference in Luke, in 2 Corinthians 12:4 when Paul spoke of a man who was "caught up in paradise," and in Revelation 2:7, where the "paradise of God" is mentioned. Paradise literally means a spacious garden. A garden is a place of growing, living things. *Heaven is not a place of eternal rest, but a place of eternal life.*

Often we wish we were not caught up in all the things we need to do and could just sit and rest. The thought is most relaxing, but if we had nothing to do and no responsibilities, living would become a bore and a burden. Paradise, the heavenly garden, is a place of beauty because it is a place of growth.

An old gospel song says it this way:*

> *We shall know...as we are known*
> *Nevermore...to walk alone...*
> *In the dawning of the morning*
> *Of that bright and happy day.*

---

*From "When the Mists Have Rolled Away" by Annie Herbert (1911).

As we think of our loved ones who have died, we are grateful for the assurance that they continue to live and that in the next life, we shall know each other.

Most of us pray, as did William Gladstone at the death of a loved one: "Dear God if he has ever been hurt by any unhappy word or deed of mine, I pray thee to heal and restore him that he might serve Thee without hindrance. Tell, him, O gracious Lord, how much I love him and miss him and long to see him again."

A little boy can walk out into the darkness without fear if he is with someone he trusts. Knowing we will be with Jesus, we need not fear death.

29

· · · · · · · · · · · ·

Faith in Life and Death

M any have said that faith in life *after* death gives one inspiration. It is much better to emphasize faith in life *and* death. We affirm life by our willingness to say yes to death. Death can be a positive encounter when we see it as an offering of our very lives to God.

One of the things that takes the desperation and isolation out of death is that it is a *shared* experience. We know that every living creature on this earth will die; we are all in this together. Furthermore, as we come closer to the experience of death, it is less frightening. We feel less resentment and anxiety as we approach the end of earthly life. We can say as others have, "My bags are all packed, and I can leave with a tranquil heart at any moment."

Most people can face the adversities of life—even death—with magnificent courage. When some loved one is facing death, the other members of the family do not need to worry about what to say or not to say. Love does not have to be expressed in words. Often just a touch or loving glance will do.

When we are forced to accept the fact of our own death, at first we may feel pain, fear, and resentment, but gradually acceptance and an almost luminous quality of joy embrace us. Percy Bysshe Shelley once wrote these words:*

Death is the veil which those who live call life: They sleep, and it is lifted.

When we have faith in life and death, we face each day, no matter what it brings, more victoriously.

---

*From "Prometheus Unbound" (1818-19).

30

. . . .

We Would Be Better Off Dead

Many of us in this country feel well off in this life. We enjoy a good quality of health, both physical and mental, our families are a source of pride and love, and we enjoy a modicum of material blessings. We look forward to the coming years of our lives; few would say we were better off dead.

Yet William Shakespeare presents a different point of view in *Hamlet*, Act III:

> *...Who would fardels [burdens] bear*
> *To grunt and sweat under a weary life,*
> *But that the dread of something after death,*
> *The undiscovered country from whose bourn*
> *No traveler returns, puzzles the will,*
> *And makes us rather bear those ills we have*
> *Than fly to others that we know not of?*

Many believe that being alive under any conditions is better than being dead. Some may agree hopeless sufferers may be better off dead, but it is normal and right to want to stay alive. We should take every care and do all we can to stay alive. It is not normal to want to die.

When one of our loved ones dies, we feel sorrow and a deep sense of loss. We think about all the things that one will be missing on this earth. We are supposed to make life the best possible and as long as possible. Life is God-given. Life is sacred. Our serious responsibility is to take care of ourselves.

However, we Christians know that really, we would be better off dead. We read, "But rather, rejoice, because your names are written in heaven" (Luke 10:20). We know Jesus has gone ahead to prepare a place for us.

When Jesus died, He cried out with a loud voice and yielded up the ghost (Matthew 27:50). What was the loud cry? Was it a cry of pain or sorrow? Perhaps, but it also could be considered a shout of victory.

Paul wrote, "For to me to live is Christ, and to

die is gain" (Philippians 1:21). Peter spoke of "an inheritance incorruptible, and undefiled, and that fadeth not away, reserved in heaven for you" (1 Peter 1:4). The physical body is not the person. The body is simply the place where the person lives while on this earth. Death releases the person from the body.

Certainly, living in the body is not bad. Here on earth we have responsibilities, a purpose to fulfill. We have work to do, loads to lift. Our duty is to work until God calls us home. The idea that we are better off dead does not mean that we are not well off now. Mortal life is good. We are to live life in the here and now as best we can. As we live here, we can experience "a foretaste of glory divine." This gives us the courage to live our best. As Charles Wesley wrote:

> *How happy every child of Grace*
> *Who know his sins forgiven!*
> *This earth, he cries, is not my place,*
> *I seek my place in heaven.*

> *A country far, from mortal sight,*
> *Which yet by faith I see*
> *The Lord of rest, the saint's delight*
> *The heaven prepared for me.*

Each of us can remember when we were away somewhere and the time came to go home. We were not sad to be going home. In fact, the best part of the journey is going home and for the Christian, death is going home.

After Benjamin Franklin's brother John died, his widow had difficulty dealing with her sorrow. Franklin wrote the following wonderful thoughts to her:

A man is not completely born until he is dead.

Why, then should we grieve that a new child is born among the unmortals. We are spirits! That temporal bodies should be lent us, while they can afford us pleasure, assist us in making a living or in acquiring knowledge, or in doing good to our fellow creatures, is a kind and benevolent act of God. When these bodies become unfit for these purposes, afford-

ing us pain instead of a blessing, it is equally kind and benevolent that God has provided a way which we can vacate them.

Death is that way. Our friend and we were invited on a path of pleasure, which is to last forever. His chair was ready first, and he is gone before us. We could not conveniently start together; and why should you and I begrieved at this, since we are soon to follow, and know where to find him.

As Susannah Wesley was dying, all her children were gathered around her bed. She said, "Children, when I am released, sing a hymn."

Believe that your loved ones who have died are truly better off dead.

31

. . . .

Is Separation Everlasting?

D eath is a time of deep sorrow and a time of separation. However, there is strengthening satisfaction in the assurance that after death, there comes a time of recognition and reunion with our loved ones.

Parents have been told when their child has died that the dear one has become an angel. This is not Scriptural. Nowhere does the Bible teach that. *Instead, parents need to know their deceased child is still their child.*

Before I was born my mother and father had a little girl who died. Her name was Ruth. Through the years they kept little Ruth's picture on the mantel in our living room. Often I would see one of them looking at that picture and wiping tears from their eyes. Even though other children were born into our home, they never gave up Ruth.

When my father died, I know he did not care whether heaven had gates of pearl or oak. It made no difference to him whether the streets were paved with gold or concrete. He wanted to see little Ruth, and if she had not been there, even heaven and all its glory would have been a disappointing place.

Truly, Robert Browning's line, "The last of life, for which the first was made," is a good description of eternity. Death does not destroy life. *Death intensifies life.* When a loved one dies, people often pray, "Lord, I believe; help thou mine unbelief" (Mark 9:24).

32

· · · · · · · · · · · ·

We Cannot Afford to Just
Go to Waste

Virtue is its own reward, someone once said. There is a reward for virtue, but if that were the only reward for our lives, it would be very little. No human virtue is great enough to bring eternal reward.

Some who are most favored in this life—who have health, wealth, earthly honor, the love of friends and family—do not understand why anyone would desire immortality. To understand, they need to consider the natural stages of life: birth, growth, decline, and death. A seed becomes a small seedling, then develops a stem, and finally produces a beautiful flower only to wilt and die after a time.

In similar fashion, people come into this life as helpless babies. Gradually their bodies develop and they become adults. They develop skills, the ability to dream and to imagine, a moral sense, and the ability to have relationships with other people. Gradually, they outgrow their bodies.

Yet as an individual becomes more spiritual, the body becomes a "socket" for the lamp of the soul. The heroic traits of people are not physical strength and brute force. Physical accomplishments are often admired and appreciated, but more important is the power of thought, of planning and of executing. We are born physical beings, but our ripeness is in our higher faculties.

As we seek to perpetuate life, we develop a powerful sense of the value of existence and a natural desire to complete unfinished things, to maintain affection for those close to us, and to continue to develop habits of enterprise. Above all, we develop the sense of value in simply being.

While an uncivilized individual or one who has received only scraps of the modern world lives for the hour, day, or year, most people live for the present and future. The Christian, however, lives with a sense of the eternal.

We cannot think of human existence without

the bright background of another life. A feeling of the continuity of existence is deeply rooted in all people.

The character we are building with so much pain and patience, with both burden and aspiration, is in our invisible souls, and is not to be blotted out by death. This assurance gives us an intrinsic sense of being somebody, of self-esteem, and influences our lives and leads us toward God.

Believing in the future, we learn to live with patience and with less and less discouragement. Paul said, "...If the dead rise not? let us eat and drink; for to morrow we die" (1 Corinthians 15:32). The attitude that life has no meaning other than the pleasure of the moment should not be acceptable.

One of the most human experiences is grief. Shocking and overwhelming, grief can even overcome faith for a moment. Grief can wreck our health and overcome our reason and moral sense. Often, though, it is in the midst of deep grief that we feel our souls crying out for immortality.

Here on this earth two people form an insepa-
rable union. They mingle their very thoughts,
share their ideals, and like flowers, grow side by
side, bringing fragrance to each other. Then comes
that moment when one dies and the other is left.
In the grief of such a wrenching experience, the
one who is left will not and cannot let go of the
hope of resurrection into a continuing life. We
do not let go of our loved ones who die. We will
not see them back on this earth, but we will see
them when we go into the next life.

33

· · · · · · · · · · ·

Worse Than Death

S ome people almost convince themselves that death is desirable. For some, dying seems an easier way out than learning how to live. It is important that we learn how to live as if death might come at any moment and work and apply ourselves as if we would live forever.

Life and death seem like opposites. But really, the faith to look at death without fear enables us to live without fear. Every living creature on earth will eventually die, but humans are the only ones who even contemplate death.

Some have expressed the thought that the Gospel writers spent too much time telling the story of Jesus' death instead of telling more about His life and teachings. However, Jesus' life and death are both one. Each sheds light on the other.

Physical life is important but the Christian faith teaches that the body is not as important as the soul. Jesus said, "And fear not them which kill the body, but are not able to kill the soul" (Matthew 10:28). If one believes that the physical life is all there is, that person's values are reversed, and he or she cannot live intelligently.

Jesus said, "Man shall not live by bread alone, but by every word of God" (Luke 4:4). A person is both physical and spiritual. Physical life is not the most important thing to a person. More important than material security is the inner power that has been given to one of God. Possessing inner power, one never depends too much on external environment and circumstances.

If all people believed it is always better to live than die, that attitude would spell the end of human nobility. Many have died because they believed some cause was more important than life. The Christian faith teaches that the death of the body is no final disaster. Jesus preferred death to compromise. For the Christian, there are some things worse than death. Death does not mean that a person is defeated.

When one betrays his or her best self for personal gain, or when one surrenders integrity for the sake of success, these may be considered worse than death. It is worse than death when one trades a clear conscience and peace of mind for physical pleasure or gain. There are many who would rather die than give up their self-respect. In addition, the betrayal of a loved one is worse than death.

What we stand for is more important than life; we must face up to our duty as human beings. Life is a matter of quality, not quantity. The kind of years is more important than the number of years.

We think the saddest death is one that comes to a child or a young person in the prime of life. However, death is even sadder for the one who was on earth for years but never really lived, one who lived without friends, or who never contributed to the world. The ultimate failure is to die without ever having committed one's life to faith in the Lord Jesus Christ.

We should be much more concerned with living life wisely and well than with simply living a long time. Paul said it magnificently: "For I am now ready to be offered, and the time of my departure is at hand. I have fought a good fight, I have finished my course, I have kept the faith: Henceforth there is laid up for me a crown of righteousness, which the Lord, the righteous judge, shall give me at that day: and not to me only, but unto all them also that love his appearing" (2 Timothy 4:6-8).

In a Roman cemetery a tombstone was seen with only these words: "I was not; I was; I am not." Most of us prefer the words of John Brown in Edwin Arlington Robinson's monologue: "I shall have more to say when I am dead."

Death is not silence and nothingness.

34

. . . .

"This World Only" Kills
Our Spirits

When we think of the length of the average life, it seems short. Many are not convinced of the importance of their lives; they feel personally insignificant.

The many things that can bring trouble or disaster to our lives—illness, accidents, crime, war—only add to the sense of futility and insecurity. The world is not a safe place to live. For many, life is like riding in a leaking boat: Even in calm seas, they must spend all their time bailing out the water.

The more things are out of control in our lives, the more we look for a higher authority to take charge. We look for something that will last, something that is the same yesterday, today, and forever.

As we grow older, we begin to realize that death is real. The older we grow, the shorter each year becomes. The second half of life goes by much faster than the first.

The tragedies of life can be overcome. A person can lose all his money and still go on living. Another can accept the fact of some physical handicap and make the necessary adjustments. But few can accept the notion that life comes to an end and there is nothing after it; this life's boundaries are not the ultimate answer. We may live on a street named Here in a city called Now, but as life goes on, we are concerned about a place named Beyond.

We live in more comfortable houses, eat better food, and enjoy more leisure activities than previous generations. We travel in planes rather than in wagons. Medical science has lengthened our expected life span. *But we will never succeed in building an earthly paradise.* Though we increase both the quantity and quality of life, this world can never provide the kind of life we deeply hunger for. This world is simply too small.

As Christians, we accept that we will die, but we don't accept that death is the end. If death were the last word, every human relationship would be lost and life itself would be trivial. If there were no sense of eternity, our souls, nurtured by the Holy Spirit, would not grow stronger as our bodies grow weaker. Because of the souls we possess within us, we are equipped for something beyond this world.

As has been well said before, we do not believe in the next life because we have proved it. Rather, we are ever trying to prove it because we believe in it.

Because of our belief in the next world, we dedicate ourselves to making this world better. We do not let the promise of "pie in the sky" keep us from acting in the interest of social justice here and now. The surer we are of forever, the less willing we are to justify the appeasement of evil on this earth. The philosophy of "this world only" does not inspire people to unselfish service to each other. We treat others with respect because they are creatures of eternity. Some say they are living in the here and now, but as we take our eyes off the next world, things go from bad to worse. This life is simply not enough.

The fact that we live forever means that the passing days are not bringing us to our doom but to fellowships that will never be broken. We are coming home after wandering in the wasteland as we witness the eternal light breaking through the darkness. Truly, "The last enemy that shall be destroyed is death" (1 Corinthians 15:26).

35

. . . .

Waking Up and Finding Heaven Is Home

The greatness and glory of heaven cannot be expressed in human language. When John had his first vision of heaven on the Isle of Patmos, he was speechless. Remember that Jesus had risen, come back to earth, and then ascended into heaven. Jesus was now speaking to John in a dream. Of his reaction to the scene in heaven, John writes, "I fell at his feet as dead" (Revelation 1:17). He was overwhelmed by what he saw.

If we could really get a vision of heaven, we, too, would be overwhelmed. Our limited capacity could not take it in for it is impossible to describe heaven in human terms.

When we attempt to describe something so wonderful and beautiful and our descriptions turn out to be completely inadequate, we use the term "heavenly." We know that heaven is fantastic, but it is not a fantasy. In referring to heaven, it is not correct to use the word "utopia" because a utopia is an imaginary and indefinitely remote place. That is not true of heaven.

God's heaven is not the same as earth. The very first book of the Bible says, "In the beginning God created the heaven and the earth" (Genesis 1:1). They are two separate and distinct places; earth is not heaven and heaven is not earth. However, it is significant that God had them in His mind together. Each supports the other. Both are real places.

When most of us think of heaven, our real interest is not so much what the place is like, but about our loved ones who are there. Heaven becomes more real and important to each of us when Mama or Papa is there.

On this earth we know our loved ones in their physical bodies. On earth the body is essential to life, but the body has many limitations. As Paul tells us, there is a "natural body." However, there is no need for a natural body beyond this world. So Paul adds: "...and there is a spiritual body" (1 Corinthians 15:44). Speaking of the spiritual body,

Jesus said, "Neither can they die any more" (Luke 20:36). We live our lives in the heavenly environment forever. We never tire of hearing the words of Paul: "To be absent from the body, and to be present with the Lord" (2 Corinthians 5:8). Life on this earth is limited; life in heaven is without limitations. As the Psalmist said, "At thy right hand there are pleasures for evermore" (Psalm 16:11).

Though we cannot see eternity with our earthly eyes, or even imagine it in our minds, we will not be surprised when we get there. C.S. Lewis has been quoted as saying that when we awaken after death, we will say, "Why, of course! Of course it's like this. How else could it have possibly been?"

Surely we will be reunited with our loved ones. Heaven has been described as the perpetual present. There are no clocks or calendars there. Change is not an experience in heaven. Our loved ones there remain the same. Concerning Lazarus, Jesus said to Martha, "Thy brother shall rise again" (John 11:23). He was still her brother even though he had died. So it is with us and our loved ones.

What a glorious thought to wake up in heaven and realize it is *home!*

36

. . . .

Do We Have Bodies After Death?

We often reflect upon our beliefs, theories, and faith in reference to eternal life. However, unless our thinking leads to some action, it is of little value. Although death will end our lives on this earth absolutely, within most people there is an "I hope" in reference to the next life. The Christian faith changes "I hope" to "I know."

In a famous passage in the *Aeneid*, Virgil used the phrase "eager longing for the further shore." But longing is not enough. *We want assurance.* We are aware of the importance of the physical body and we know there comes that time when our soul does more than soar into spiritual freedom. We know the physical body is not the enemy of the soul.

Speaking of the body in relation to the experience of death, Paul said, "It is sown in corruption: it is raised in incorruption. It is sown in dishonour; it is raised in glory: it is sown in weakness; it is raised in power: It is sown a natural body; it is raised a spiritual body" (1 Corinthians 15:42-44). Yes, in the next life we do have bodies.

The Christian view holds out the prospect of a life where the noblest qualities of the human soul come into their own. After death we are given another chance for the fulfillment of the best in the individual life. Eternal life overcomes all human limitations.

When we stand at the grave of a loved one, we know that the grave is not the end. Some say that upon death "the bottle is poured back into the ocean" but that is not true. An unknown poet once wrote these words:

> *Thou wilt not leave us in the dust.*
> *Thou madest man, he knows not why.*
> *He thinks he was not made to die.*
> *And Thou has made him: Thou art just.*

Some may suggest we think too much of the

"by and by" and forget about the "here and now."
However, instead of the idea of eternal life turning our attention away from earthly life, we should realize it gives more meaning to this life. *Eternity gives purpose to the earthly*. Eternity bestows dignity and meaning upon this present life. Character becomes the chief concern of this life. The truth of immortality makes for great living.

When someone asks, "How can the assurance of eternal life become mine?" there is, ultimately, but one answer. "I am the resurrection, and the life: he that believeth in me,... shall never die" (John 11:25, 26).

37

. . . .

Four Reasons We Fear Death

G enerally speaking, people want to live, and there are at least four reasons why.

First, death seems like stepping off the edge of a precipice in a dense fog into the unknown. Our minds cannot imagine such a situation. Job refers to the next life as "the land of darkness" (Job 10:21).

However, as the Christian faces death, there is one Face that can be seen. The Face of Christ brightens the doom. The known Christ filling the unknown makes the difference.

Second, death seems hostile because we feel it takes us away from the activities of this life and into a state of inaction. For most people, the activities and occupations of this life are desirable. Retirement is not something to look forward to if there is nothing to do. The thought of eternal rest is boring.

But death is the opposite of retiring. Jesus has

made a promise to those who are faithful in this life: "Well done, good and faithful servant; thou hast been faithful over a few things, I will make thee ruler over many things: enter thou into the joy of thy lord" (Matthew 25:23). Death is the emancipation of the soul into greater activity.

Third, death causes separation from our loved ones. At the same time, however, death unites us with all those who have gone on before. We realize the separation on this earth is temporary. The ones we are leaving will follow. Death is the supreme uniter.

Finally, after death the judgment will occur. The thought of having to face up to everything in our past can be frightening as well as shameful. But our trust is not in ourselves. Our trust is in Jesus because, believing in Him, we are promised that we will not "perish, but have everlasting life" (John 3:16). We remember the words of the prophet: "Though your sins be as scarlet, they shall be as white as snow; though they be red like crimson, they shall be as wool" (Isaiah 1:18).

When we die, we come to the "iron gate that leadeth unto the city; which opened to them of his own accord" (Acts 12:10).

38

. . . .

When a Loved One Has Died

The death of a loved one brings deep and abiding sorrow. In the darkness of the experience, sorrow can find the light and keep us going. Sorrow reveals to us our inner strength given to us by God and shows us new meanings in life.

Many of us try not to think about the death of a dear one. We want to keep it as hidden as possible. When others seek to comfort us, we do not want the name of our loved one mentioned. When we look at a loved one in a casket, the expression we are wont to use is, "He looks so natural."

Many do not want to use the word "died;" we use such euphemisms as "passed on," "entered into eternal rest," "gone to be with the Lord," or even "expired."

To keep from facing the fact of death, we practice many forms of self-deception and denial.

Yet the death of a loved one brings us face-to-

221

face with immortality. Death is not the final chapter in the drama of life. We continue to love the one who has died. This love is not just part of our memories but continues because we believe that life is ongoing. We feel deep sorrow over the end of the physical presence, but we take great comfort over the assurance of eternity.

Alfred, Lord Tennyson wrote these words:*

> *Twilight and evening bell,*
> *And after that the dark.*
> *And may there be no sadness of farewell*
> *When I embark;*
> *For though from out our home of time and place*
> *The blood may bear me far*
> *I hope to see my Pilot face to face*
> *When I have crossed the bar.*

Death makes the words of the Psalmist very real: "And I will dwell in the house of the Lord forever" (Psalm 23:6). There is deep and abiding solace that comes from our belief that life continues. We never realize the joy of that belief until

*From "Crossing the Bar" (1889).

we face the reality of death. To quote the Psalmist again, "The Lord preserveth all them that love
him" (Psalm 145:20).

We do not need to be overcome by foolish regrets as we mourn a loved one. Of course, we
can remember when either we or they did not
properly measure up. It is normal to wish something had been different or had not happened.
But after a loved one has entered into eternal life,
our regrets and guilt should be forgotten. We need
to remember and dwell on the larger part of the
relationship and the happy times and love we
shared. Our loved ones would not want to be remembered with vain regrets.

Although the sorrow of separation is natural
and normal, it is a blessed truth that in our hearts
our loved ones never die. Love continues to hold
us together.

The poet Mary Lee Hall, in her poem "Solace,"
said it beautifully:

> *If I should die and leave you here a while,*
> *Be not like others, sore undone, who keep*

Long vigil by the silent dust and weep.
For my sake turn again to life and smile.

There is comfort in the words, "Death came as a friend." When we think of the infirmities of age, the pain and suffering of the body, the storms and struggles of life, we can take comfort knowing that death opens the portals to a life free from all troubles. If we truly know and believe this, we would not bring our loved ones back even if we could.

Often there are not words sufficient to meet our grief, hurt, and disappointment. There is, however, one consolation: For some, the door opens sooner to eternal life.

Let us believe that when death comes, and it will come sooner or later to every living being, we can be assured it will come as a friend who lovingly leads us to our eternal home, *heaven.* That is the good news about heaven.

ISBN 1-55748-599-2

90000

9 781557 485991